Computer
NETWORKS

Clive Gifford

Crabtree Publishing Company

www.crabtreebooks.com

Crabtree Publishing Company
www.crabtreebooks.com
1-800-387-7650

Published in Canada
Crabtree Publishing
616 Welland Ave.
St. Catharines, ON
L2M 5V6

Published in the United States
Crabtree Publishing
PMB 59051, 350 Fifth Ave.
59th Floor,
New York, NY

First published in 2015 by Wayland
(A division of Hachette Children's Books)
Copyright © Wayland 2015

Author: Clive Gifford
Commissioning editor: Debbie Foy
Project editor: Caroline West (Blue Dragonfly Ltd.)
Editorial director: Kathy Middleton
Project coordinator: Kelly Spence
Editor: Petrina Gentile
Consultant: Lee Martin, B. Ed
Designer: Mark Latter (Blue Dragonfly Ltd.)
Proofreader: Shannon Welbourn
Prepress technician: Margaret Amy Salter
Print and production coordinator: Margaret Amy Salter

Printed in Canada/022015/MA20150101

Photographs:
All images courtesy of Shutterstock

While every attempt has been made to clear
copyright, should there be any inadvertent
omission this will be rectified in future editions.

Disclaimer: The website addresses (URLs)
included in this book were valid at the time
of going to press. However, because of the
nature of the Internet, it is possible that some
addresses may have changed, or sites may have
changed or closed down since publication.
While the author and publisher regret any
inconvenience this may cause the readers, no
responsibility for any such changes can be
accepted by either the author or the publisher.
Note to reader: Words highlighted in bold
appear in the Glossary on page 30.
Answers to activities are on page 31.

Library and Archives Canada Cataloguing in Publication

Gifford, Clive, author
    Computer networks / Clive Gifford.

(Get connected to digital literacy)
Includes index.
Issued in print and electronic formats.
ISBN 978-0-7787-1509-2 (bound).--ISBN 978-0-7787-1560-3
(pbk.).--
ISBN 978-1-4271-1586-7 (pdf).--ISBN 978-1-4271-1582-9 (html)

    1. Computer networks--Juvenile literature. I. Title.

TK5105.5.G53 2015   j004.6   C2014-908283-5
                                          C2014-908284-3

Library of Congress Cataloging-in-Publication Data

Gifford, Clive, author.
    Computer networks / Clive Gifford.
        pages cm. -- (Get connected to digital literacy)
    Includes index.
    ISBN 978-0-7787-1509-2 (reinforced library binding : alk. paper)
    -- ISBN 978-0-7787-1560-3 (pbk. : alk. paper) --
    ISBN 978-1-4271-1586-7 (electronic pdf : alk. paper) --
    ISBN 978-1-4271-1582-9 (electronic html : alk. paper)
    1. Computer networks--Juvenile literature. 2. World Wide Web--
Juvenile literature. 3. Information technology--Juvenile literature.
I. Title.

TK5105.5.G525 2015
004.6--dc23
                                2014048907

Contents

Making Connections

A computer network is a way for computers and other devices to connect with each other. This enables them to communicate using special rules to share data, information, and resources.

⬇ It's a revolution

The first computer networks were created in the 1960s when huge military and university computers were joined together to share technical information. No one at the time knew where this would lead.

Even just 25 years ago, no one used computer networks except at work, but now they're everywhere. Computer networks allow people to look at websites on smartphones or tablets, send and receive emails, do their banking, shop, and work from home, as well as **stream** videos and music from anywhere in the world onto a digital device such as a Smart TV.

All over the world

Computer networks can help people stay connected. For example, in Japan and Australia, thousands of school children are taught over the **Internet** by teachers who live hundreds of miles away. Millions of people run businesses from home and connect with the world using computer networks.

TRUE STORY

Out Of This World Computer networks have even left Earth and now provide network links in space. In 2010, astronauts on the International Space Station, whizzing high above Earth at a speed of 17,150 mph (27,600 km/h), got their own computer network link. This allows them to view websites and send messages.

NASA astronauts in space even have their own Twitter account. You can view their messages and out-of-this-world photographs by typing the following link into a web browser:

http://twitter.com/NASA_Astronauts

5

Networks in Action

Computer networks allow hundreds of millions of people around the world to use computers to share information, learn, and be entertained. Here are just some of the many different things you can do using a computer network.

Explore, discover, learn
All sorts of facts can be at your fingertips over a computer network. You can read newspapers, books and magazines—all on screen.

Read a map
Out and about? Maps sent over a computer network to a smartphone or tablet can tell you precisely where you are and where to go next.

TRUE STORY

Get Elected In 2007, Estonia became the first country in the world to choose its government by people voting over the Internet using computers.

Shop online

Many people do their grocery shopping or order meals over the Internet without having to leave home. They do this using debit or credit cards instead of cash. The first ever delivery order was made in 1994 on PizzaNet. It was for a pepperoni and mushroom pizza with extra cheese.

Play games

Lots of games can be played over computer networks against other people—even if they are in different parts of the world. For example, in 2013, the game World of Warcraft was played by over seven million people from more than 150 countries!

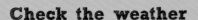

Listen to podcasts

You can listen to digital recordings called **podcasts** that are downloaded over a computer network. You only need a microphone, a computer, and some programs to make your own podcast.

Check the weather

Up-to-the-minute weather forecasts are available from websites, which users can check on a tablet or smartphone.

Let's Connect

Computers have to connect to a network so that they can work with other devices. Some networks are wired with each device being joined by a cable. Wireless networks use radio waves or satellite signals to link devices.

 ## LAN plan

LAN is short for Local Area Network. A LAN is made up of lots of computers that are linked together over a short distance. You may have a LAN at home. A **router** connects a home network to the Internet, which is usually received over a phone or cable line. Computers and other devices are linked by cables plugged into the router or link to it wirelessly.

 ## Wide area networks

WANs are Wide Area Networks that work over long distances. For example, the bank machines that give out cash to customers are linked in WANs so that people can use them all over a country or even a continent.

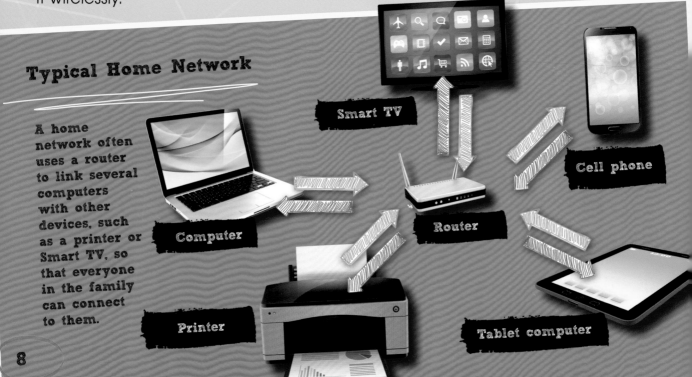

Typical Home Network

A home network often uses a router to link several computers with other devices, such as a printer or Smart TV, so that everyone in the family can connect to them.

Smart TV

Cell phone

Computer

Router

Printer

Tablet computer

Satellite Connection

In remote places, where there aren't any phone lines, people can still access computer networks using a space **satellite**. Even scientists and explorers at the South Pole can surf websites and send emails using a satellite Internet link.

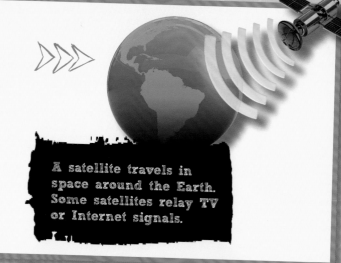

A satellite travels in space around the Earth. Some satellites relay TV or Internet signals.

 ## Look, no wires, it's Wi-Fi

Wi-Fi lets devices, such as tablets and smartphones, connect wirelessly to computer networks. A Wi-Fi transmitter sends out information from the Internet as radio signals that other devices with Wi-Fi, such as a phone, printer, or computer, can pick up. The area around the transmitter in which devices can use Wi-Fi is called a **hotspot**. This allows people to stay connected when on the move. Where two or more devices create a network using Wi-Fi, a Wireless Local Area Network (WLAN) is made.

 ## Cloud computing

You can store your documents and images on a computer away from your own. This not only frees up space inside your own computer, it also means you can access your data using the Internet from a different computer or digital device. This is known as cloud computing.

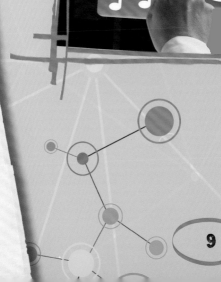

TRUE STORY

That's So Slow! In early home computer networking, people put a telephone into a machine called an acoustic coupler. This sent signals down the phone line and was usually very slow. A music track that only takes a minute to download today would take more than two days using an acoustic coupler.

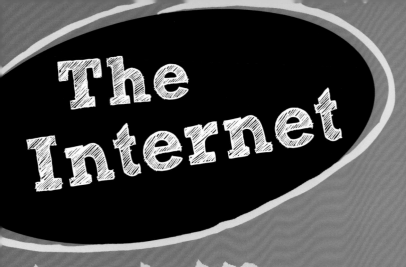

The Internet

The Internet is the world's biggest computer network. It is made up of lots of smaller networks that span the globe. These link all sorts of different computers and devices, including games, consoles, phones, and even fridges.

⬇ Where did it all begin?

The Internet developed out of ARPANET (Advanced Research Projects Agency Network), an early network in the United States that let scientists and military forces share information. The number of people who owned or had access to a personal computer boomed from the late 1980s onwards. This meant that more people began to use **modems** to connect their computers to the Internet. New uses for these connected computers were developed, including the World Wide Web and email. In 1985, there were less than 5,000 computers linked to the Internet. Today, there are an estimated 15 billion computers, smartphones, tablets, and other machines able to access the Internet.

This picture shows some of the different connection paths of Internet traffic across Europe.

TRUE STORY

Submerged! There are more than 497,000 miles (800,000km) of underwater cables carrying Internet data across seas and oceans. That's enough to circle the Earth 20 times.

Connecting to the net

You can connect to the Internet in different ways. Some people pay an **ISP** or Internet Service Provider to give them a connection, either through a cable run into their home, over a telephone line, or via a satellite connection.

Internet cafés have computers that are connected to the Internet. Other places have Wi-Fi hotspots that let people with Wi-Fi devices, such as tablets or smartphones, access the Internet.

Remote Connections

Millions of people around the world do not have access to the Internet because they are without any electricity. One clever scheme to help them is the ZubaBox. Large shipping containers are used to house computers. These are powered by solar panels on the roofs. The containers are shipped to remote places in the world such as parts of Africa.

In areas of Nepal, people in some villages are more than two days' walk from an Internet connection. So, local man Mahabir Pun began collecting old, unwanted computers and junk parts to build homemade Internet connections. Mahabir has now helped more than 170 villages in Nepal gain Internet access.

Internet cafés allow people to connect with and use the Internet when away from home or work.

11

World Wide Web

In 1990, a computer was switched on in Switzerland and a revolution began. The computer was the first web server and the World Wide Web was born. By the start of 2014, there were over 250 million websites!

Clicking on a hyperlink takes you from one web page to another.

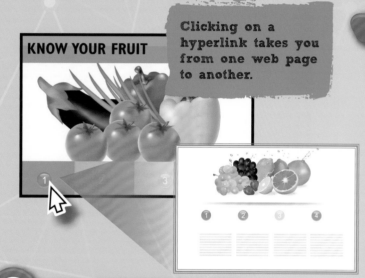

All linked together

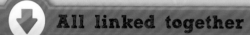

The World Wide Web is also known as WWW or the "web." It is a HUGE collection of websites that you can look at using the Internet. Each website is made of **web pages**. Some websites only have a single page, but others contain hundreds. Each web page is connected to others by **hyperlinks**, which can be text or pictures.

Browsing around

To look at pages on the web, your computer device needs a special program called a web browser. When you make a search or type in a link, the browser asks a **web server** for the pages. It then receives and displays the pages over the Internet.

1. A tablet runs a web browser program.

2. The web browser connects to a web server and asks for a page.

3. The web server computer stores web pages.

4. The web server sends back the page, which is shown on the screen.

SURFING THE WEB

Popular web browser programs include Google Chrome, Safari, Internet Explorer, and Mozilla Firefox.

There is an address bar at the top of most web browsers. This is where you can type in the web address (see page 15) of the web page you would like to view.

The back button takes you to the previous page you looked at.

The forward button takes you to the page you were on before pressing the back button.

The home button takes you to the first page you see when you open a web browser.

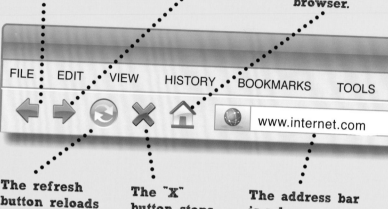

FILE   EDIT   VIEW   HISTORY   BOOKMARKS   TOOLS   HELP

www.internet.com

The refresh button reloads the web page that you are viewing.

The "X" button stops a web page loading.

The address bar is where you type the address or URL of the website you want to visit.

COMPUTER Hero!

Tim Berners-Lee started out as a computer scientist. He was interested in using hyperlinks to connect different documents to make it easier for people to share their work.

So, Tim created **HTML** (see page 14) to make the first ever website.

He also invented the first web browser and **HTTP**—this is a set of rules that lets all computers use hyperlinked documents over the Internet.

Type http://info.cern.ch into a web browser to see the first ever website made by Tim Berners-Lee.

Tim Berners-Lee

Web Wonders

Web pages and websites have to be created by web designers first before they can be stored on a web server. From here, they can reach the World Wide Web where people can view and use them.

Tagging text

Most web pages are created using a language called Hypertext Markup Language or HTML. This is used to mark up documents with special codes called tags so that they can become web pages.

The first web pages only contained letters and numbers, but today sound files, photographs, animated cartoons, and colorful backgrounds can all be added. Here are two examples of HTML tags:

\<u\>This text is underlined\</u\> while \<b\>this text is bold.\</b\>

This \<u\> tag will underline the text that follows it.

This is a closing tag, ending the effect.

This tag turns the text bold.

A closing tag always contains a backslash.

<u>This text is underlined</u> while **this text is bold.**

STRETCH YOURSELF

Explore HTML

 You can look at HTML codes in action by visiting a web page, right-clicking on your mouse or hold down the control key and click a Mac's one-button mouse. Select "view" or "show page source" from the menu of options that pops up. If you are unsure, ask an adult to help you.

 Explore the W3 Schools website to see how HTML codes are used to mark up text for a website. Just type the following into your web browser:

www.w3schools.com/html/html_examples.asp

WHAT'S THE ADDRESS?

So, how does a web server know which web page to send to your device? That's the job of something called an Uniform Resource Locator or **URL**. This acts as a web address. Every web page has its own unique URL so that it can be found easily on the World Wide Web.

http
(Hypertext Transfer Protocol) is the format used to send data over the Internet.

www
This stands for World Wide Web.

Domain name
This is usually the full or shortened name of the organization.

Index
This identifies the specific web page you are looking for.

http://www.worldwildlife.org/places/the-galapagos

Domain type
This shows who runs the website. Here are some more examples:

.com = commerical
.edu = educational
.gov = government
.org = organization

Country code
This often appears after the domain type. It tells you what country the website is from. Here are some more examples:

.uk = United Kingdom   .us = United States
.fr = France   .cn = China
.it = Italy   .pe = Peru
.de = Germany   .ca = Canada
.au = Australia

 Favorite places

If you really like a web page, then click on the favorites or bookmarks button in your browser. This will save a web page's address in the browser program so that you can find it quickly the next time you are on the web.

 Up to the minute

Once a web page has been made, it is sent to a web server. This is called **uploading**. Unlike printed newspapers and books, web pages can be updated and re-uploaded many times a day.

A World of Websites

There are websites on all sorts of subjects, from aardvarks to sharks! Governments and organizations, for example, use websites to provide advice. People also create websites about their hobbies.

Libraries online

Libraries, museums, and other organizations, such as the United Nations and National Geographic, produce helpful websites that are packed with information on a wide range of topics. These are often very good places to learn about a subject.

STRETCH YOURSELF

Find the Facts

The American Library Association's Great Websites for Kids is a fantastic place to find information. Visit the website by typing the following link into your web browser:

http://gws.ala.org/

☞ Can you find out how many different subject categories the websites are divided into?

☞ Try to find some websites about butterflies, dinosaurs, or space.

Answer on page 31

Sharing your thoughts

A **blog** or web log is a diary or journal that a person puts on the World Wide Web. Blogs can be full of opinions and lots of fun, but are not always as accurate for facts as information websites.

Anyone can write a blog. For example, nine-year-old Martha Payne started a blog about school dinners called "NeverSeconds" in 2012. Within a year, her blog had been read 10 million times and helped raise over $187,500 for a charity aiming to make sure all school children have enough food.

Buying and selling

Many websites are built by companies to sell goods or services. This is called **e-commerce**. One of the biggest e-commerce companies is Amazon. On December 2, 2013, Amazon sold an amazing 36.8 million items in one day. That's about 426 items every second!

COMPUTER Heroes!

Chad Hurley, Steve Chen, and **Jawed Karim** built a website so that people could share their videos. In 2005, the first video of Jawed visiting a zoo went on the website. It was only 18 seconds long. YouTube had begun!

Chad Hurley and Steve Chen

OFFENSIVE WEBSITES!

There are some websites that you may find upsetting. Make sure someone has set search filters on your computer to "safe search" and tell an adult immediately if you spot anything you don't like.

Search Engines

The amount of information on the World Wide Web is really mind-boggling. Some websites contain hundreds or thousands of web pages. Search engines sift through these pages to help you find the information you want.

Using search engines

There are lots of popular search engines, such as Yahoo, Bing, and Google, as well as special ones for children such as KidRex and KidsClick. Most search engines ask you to type in search terms or keywords to find what you are looking for. In the blink of an eye, they then return a list of results—usually web pages. Each item in the list is hyperlinked so that you can click on it to visit that web page.

Spiders on the Web

Behind each search engine on the World Wide Web are a number of computer programs that do the hard work.

1) Search engines send out programs called spiders or crawlers. These travel around the World Wide Web and make lists of the words and pictures they find on different web pages.

2) The lists are filed by programs called indexers and then stored in a giant computer database.

3) When you search for something on the World Wide Web, the search engine quickly looks through its giant database to find matches.

4) The search engine then displays the results in the order it thinks is the most important.

COMPUTER Heroes!

Sergey Brin and **Larry Page** built a search engine called BackRub when they were students, which eventually became Google. In 2013, over 5.9 billion searches were carried out on Google every day!

STRETCH YOURSELF

Can You Search Smartly?

Practice searching for information on the World Wide Web by trying these challenges.

 Use the search engines for kids listed below to find out about:

Steve Jobs

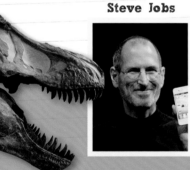

Dinosaur skeletons

The Sphinx of Ancient Egypt

www.kidsclick.org/index.php
www.awesomelibrary.org/
www.kidrex.org/

What have you found out?

☞ Check out your searching skills by using the KidRex search engine to answer this question:

Which travels faster: the fastest sofa on wheels or a cheetah?

Cheetah

Fastest sofa on wheels

www.kidrex.org/

HELPFUL TIP!
Try searching for words such as top speed, fastest sofa, and world record.

Answer on page 31

19

Search and Filter

There are so many websites on the Internet that search engines often return thousands of results. You cannot read all these web pages, so you need to find ways to search smartly and filter your results.

It's a word game

Try to use a number of words in your search. If one set of words doesn't give you the right results, try other similar words. Always check your spelling when typing in search terms. For example, searching for "brakefast" and "breakfast" will give two very different sets of search results!

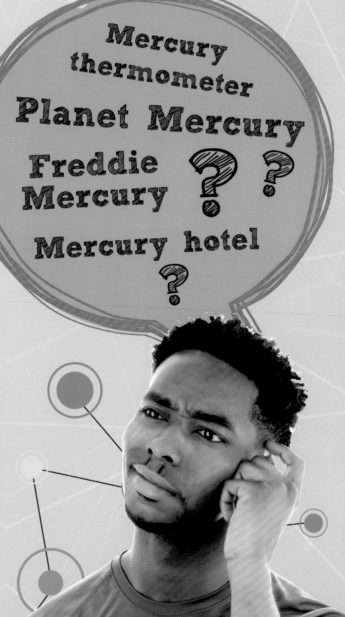

Mercury thermometer
Planet Mercury
Freddie Mercury
Mercury hotel

What's in a name?

Even a word spelled correctly can have different meanings. For instance, if you are searching for facts about the metal mercury, include metal in your search terms. Just typing in "mercury" will give lots of results about the planet Mercury, the Mercury Spacecraft, and newspapers and hotels called Mercury.

Making your mark

You can use quotation marks to make a search engine look for an exact phrase. This can be helpful when you are looking for films, books, or phrases that contain short words, or numbers such as "the" or "two," which most search engines ignore.

Typing "American Civil War" should only return results about that war and not other civil wars.

Clever searching

A minus sign is a handy tool that can be used to avoid certain results. If you want to search for information about the city of Chicago, for example, but not its baseball team, then you could type in "Chicago–baseball."

FIRST ISN'T ALWAYS BEST

Not everything on the World Wide Web is true or up-to-date, so always be careful when you are searching for information. Here are some things to keep in mind:

* How old is the web page? See if there is a date when the web page was created. Some subjects, such as world records, sports, news, and science change fast.

* Who made the web page? Is it an individual, a company, or a trusted organization such as a museum or an encyclopedia?

* Don't only look at the first few search results. Compare the facts on different web pages.

Don't Be Fooled!

Facts on websites aren't always true. In 2012, a story and photograph about a giant Amazonian tortoise, which was four times the size of a person, appeared on websites. But this was a trick! The picture was from a Japanese science fiction movie called *Gamera the Brave*.

You've Got Mail

Electronic mail, or email, is a type of message sent over a computer network. Emails only take a moment to reach their target, no matter where in the world they are sent.

 Getting mail

To send and receive emails, you can either install an email program on your computer or use a web-based email service. This alerts you when emails arrive and lets you write and send emails as well. Most programs let you save emails and delete those that you don't want anymore.

 Address success

Just like a letter or postcard, an email needs an address. An email address has two parts, which are separated by an @, or at, symbol. The first part is chosen by the email account holder. The second part after the @ is the domain or host name. This is the company, perhaps Gmail or Hotmail, who provide the email service.

This is where you type the person's email address.

This button lets you send attachments.

B I U

To: name@here.com

Subject: **Happy Holidays!**

Remember to say what your email is about in the subject line.

Hello Grandma,

Hope you have a great holiday!

Love Sophie x

This is where you type your message. Always start with a greeting and finish with a good-bye and your name.

! **Warning:** Guard your email address carefully—don't give it to strangers.

Attach that

Along with the text in your email, you can also attach files. The attachment might be a photograph, an essay, or letter, or a sound file.

However, you need to be very careful when opening any attachments that come with the emails you receive. This is because the attachments might contain computer **viruses** that will harm your computer (see pages 26–27).

(see pages 26–27)

TRUE STORY

Space Mail The first email from space was sent in 1991 by the crew of the Space Shuttle Atlantis. It read:

 "Hello Earth! Greetings from the STS-43 Crew… Having a GREAT time, wish you were here!"

STRETCH YOURSELF

Mail a Tale
Why not write a group story by email? Let each person take turns writing a few lines of the story before emailing it to the next person in the group to add a few more lines.

☞ Ask an adult to show you how to save each email so that you can keep track of the story.

☞ How long can you make your story last?

☞ Can you email each other with ideas for how the story should end?

Happy or sad?

Want to get across how you feel quickly in an email? You can use little faces with expressions called emoticons. Many email programs contain emoticons for you to add to your messages.

Social Networks

People love to chat and share information, tell stories, and talk about things that interest them. Social networking lets people from all over the world connect over computer networks.

Social media

People use social networking websites such as Facebook and Twitter to keep in touch. Facebook users create a profile, then they can link up with friends, play games, and share information. Twitter lets people send **tweets** to everyone that follows them. Twitter users can also follow other people and receive their tweets. Jokes, opinions, and news are the most common topics for tweets.

We love to talk!

Some social media sites, such as Snapchat, WhatsApp, and Instagram are designed for sharing photographs and videos. Tumblr is a social network for people to write and share blogs. Pinterest lets you use virtual pinboards to share pictures and ideas with others.

Different interests

Some social networks are for people with special interests. Goodreads, for example, lets people share their love of books. LinkedIn has over 200 million members who list their work skills and experience, and use the network to contact business colleagues.

Netiquette

You need to be nice and polite when communicating with other people on the Internet. Social networks only work well when everyone is friendly and fair to each other. If someone doesn't agree with you or is rude on a social network, don't get angry or try to get even. Walk away from your computer or phone and do something fun until you've calmed down.

You also might want to avoid typing anything in CAPITAL LETTERS. This might suggest to others that you are VERY ANGRY and so should be avoided.

Mark Zuckerberg originally created "thefacebook" in 2004 so students at Harvard University in the United States could share information about each other. By 2006, Facebook had 12 million members. By 2014, it had over one billion!

Mark Zuckerberg

UNSOCIAL NETWORKS

Most social networks, including Facebook and Instagram, only allow adults and older children to take part. This is because, sadly, some people on social networks may be rude, say horrible things, or send upsetting pictures. If you read or see anything that upsets you, let an adult know at once.

TRUE STORY

Top Tweeters Pop stars have the most Twitter followers. Lady Gaga, Justin Bieber, Katy Perry, and Taylor Swift have over 40 million followers each!

25

Danger, Danger!

Going online can be lots of fun, but there are dangers ahead if you are not careful. Here are some of the threats to you and your computer that exist online.

Computer viruses

A computer virus is a piece of computer code that can copy itself and damage your computer if, for example, you open an email attachment by mistake. A virus might be a prank and just display a joke or rude message. However, other viruses can make your computer perform slowly or stop working altogether. Some viruses will even start to wipe all the data from a computer's hard disk.

Trojan horse programs are named after an old Greek legend where soldiers hide inside a wooden horse to surprise their enemy!

Beat the virus!

Anti-virus software are programs that detect and, in most cases, remove viruses and other security threats. Most spot viruses by comparing the files on a computer to a database of known viruses.

Trojan horses

Trojan horses are programs, such as free games, that are disguised to look safe. However, once one of these programs runs on your computer, it can break its security, which means that other harmful programs such as viruses can infect it.

Like living viruses that make you feel sick some computer viruses may damage your computer.

Email Virus In 2004, the MyDoom virus hid in email attachments. When the email was opened, the virus ran on the computer and sent emails containing copies of itself to all the addresses on the computer. Around two million computers were infected in a few weeks.

Spyware

These programs record what you type or what you do on your computer. Some spyware is designed to steal your passwords or personal details. Anti-spyware programs can detect and remove spyware.

COMPUTER Hero!

In the 1980s, **John McAfee's** computer was infected with a virus. McAfee was a computer programmer and could easily remove the virus, but he thought other people might struggle. So, in 1987, he wrote the first major anti-virus program called VirusScan.

EMAIL DANGERS!

* Don't open or answer emails if they are from people you don't know or trust.

* Don't open attachments or downloads if you don't know what they are. These could contain upsetting messages or images, or computer viruses.

* Don't reply to emails asking for personal details such as your name, address, and birthday because they might be from a fake company.

Keep it to Yourself

Most people using the Internet are nice and friendly, but some may use your personal information against you. This is why you should always guard your data carefully and never share it online.

That's personal

Your full name, address, phone number, and the school you go to are all examples of personal data. So are details of your family members and what jobs they do. Your personal data also includes the passwords you use to gain access to websites and other places on the Internet.

Leaving footprints

Your digital footprint is all the information that can be found about you on social networks, websites, in emails, and other places. It not only includes all the things you have typed, but may also include photographs and things that have been typed about you by others. This is why you need to be careful what you do and say online.

Password Protection

Some people use weak passwords and never change them. This makes it easy for other people to guess what they are. Here are some obvious passwords that anyone could crack:

The first six letters on the top row of a keyboard.

1. 123456
2. password
3. qwerty
4. abc123

Create a strong password by using a short word or phrase you will remember and disguise it with a random mix of upper and lower case letters, numbers, and symbols. For example, zebra could be Ze6RrA and Los Angeles could be L0s(nGe7es.

Staying Safe

Keep it secret
Don't tell other people your passwords and make sure you have strong passwords that are not easy to guess.

Careful how you go
Stick to trusted websites that are suitable for your age and interests. Never give out information that you wouldn't be happy to share with everyone. Never pass on hurtful messages or photos about others, as you could be helping cyber bullies.

Stranger danger
Never agree to see a stranger that you have met on the Internet. Don't send photographs of yourself either. This is because people are not always who they pretend to be. Some are adults pretending to be kids.

Cyber bullying
Bullying doesn't only happen at school and other physical places; it can also happen over computer networks. If you feel bullied, don't respond to the upsetting messages, save them as evidence and let a trusted adult know.

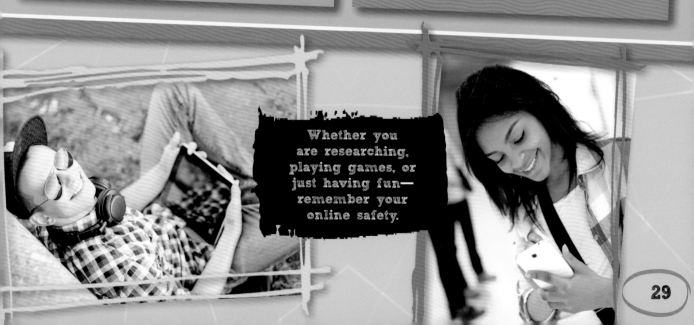

Whether you are researching, playing games, or just having fun— remember your online safety.

Glossary

blog Short for web log, this is a list of diary or journal entries posted on a web page for others to read. Many people find blogging a simple way to publish views, opinions, and stories over computer networks

e-commerce Buying and selling, as well as other business transactions, which are conducted by people and companies over a computer network

hotspot A place where you can use a tablet, smartphone, or computer to connect to the Internet using a wireless connection

HTML (HyperText Markup Language) A type of language for writing web pages so that they can be displayed on different devices using the Internet

HTTP (HyperText Transfer Protocol) A set of rules that allows computer data and files to be transferred on the World Wide Web

hyperlink A word, phrase, or image on a web page that when clicked on allows the user to jump to a new place in the website or another web page

Internet A network that connects millions of computers all over the world

ISP (Internet Service Provider) A company or organization that provides users with a way of connecting to the Internet

modem An electronic device that allows computers to connect over a network, and send and receive digital data

podcast A series of audio files that people can access or download using the Internet and then listen to

router A device that takes information from a computer network and delivers it to different computers or digital devices

satellite A machine traveling around the Earth in space that performs useful work. Some satellites relay TV or Internet signals to different parts of the planet

spider (or crawler) A computer program that searches through the World Wide Web collecting details of web pages for search engines

stream To send a constant flow of data over a computer network to play music or show a video

tweet A message of no more than 140 characters that people post on the social networking site Twitter

upload To send a computer file from one computer to another or, if connected to a network, posting the file on the network for others to share, view, and use

URL (Uniform Resource Locator) A unique address for each file or web page held on a computer network such as the Internet

virus A type of computer program that can make copies of itself and runs on a computer without your permission

web page A document that is found on the World Wide Web

web server A computer that stores and serves up or delivers web pages to viewers when they are connected to the Internet and make a request

Wi-Fi Wireless local area network technology that allows people to connect computers and other digital devices to each other and to the Internet

Further Resources

Books

Understanding Computer Networks by Matthew Anniss (Heinemann-Raintree, 2015)

How Does a Network Work? by Matthew Anniss (Gareth Stevens, 2014)

Safe Social Networking by Barbara Linde (Gareth Stevens, 2013)

Websites

http://kidshealth.org/teen/safety/safebasics/internet_safety.html
A helpful guide to staying safe on the Internet and World Wide Web.

www.brainpop.com/technology/computerscience/cloudcomputing/preview.weml
Find out how cloud computing works and why it is so useful.

www.carnegiecyberacademy.com/
Fun games and lots of tips for keeping safe when using computers.

Answers

page 16 Find the Facts:
* The Great Website for Kids is divided into 8 subjects (Animals, The Arts, History & Biography, Literature & Languages, Mathematics & Computers, Reference Desk, Sciences, and Social Sciences).

page 19 Can You Search Smartly?:
The fastest sofa on wheels is faster than a cheetah!

(www.engadget.com/2007/05/16/sofa-sets-new-land-speed-record-for-furniture/)